About You
Write
Your Memoir

Jan Holmes Frost

About You - Your Memoir

BISAC Subject Headings:

BIO026000 BIOGRAPHY & AUTOBIOGRAPHY/Personal Memoirs
FAM046000 FAMILY & RELATIONSHIPS/Life Stages/General
FIC041000 FICTION/Biographical

For information write to:
RimeQuillPub@gmail.com

Visit:
www.janholmesfrost.com

ISBN: 978-0-9988-709-6-0 Print
ISBN: 978-0-9988-709-7-7 eBook

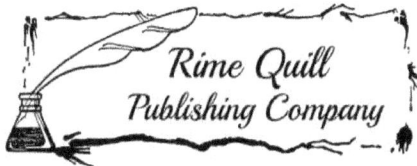

Rime Quill
Publishing Company

TABLE OF CONTENTS

Lesson 1 – An Academy Award

"There is no greater agony than bearing an untold story inside you."
Maya Angelou

You've lived a story book life worthy of a Motion Picture Academy Award. Well maybe not that big, but who knows...the tiniest snapshot of one's life can speak volumes.

Think about it this way...you know your story. Does anyone else? Perhaps someone, a friend or relative, shares a snippet with you, but not the entire tale. When your thoughts return to these snippets, there is no doubt in your mind **the story has to be told**!

How many times a week do some of these (we'll call them 'chunks') chunks of your life pop back into your mind? In all these years have they ever stopped pestering you? And when these chunks appear, do you say... **'I've got to write it down'**?

The question that begs to be answered...**If you don't write it, who will?** How do you feel when you realize these chunks will die with you if you don't take action? Here is an interesting quote:

"Don't die with your MUSIC still in you."

Wayne Dyer

"Don't die with your STORY still in you!"   *Me*

Yes I'm using scare tactics…if this is what it takes to get you to share your story with the world (or at least with your family). What do I first hear from people with stories to be told…?

"I don't know where or how to begin."

"It's too overwhelming."

"We're talking so many years!"

"My memory is failing me, I'd never get it right after all this time."

"I don't even know how to use a computer."

"How do I start?"

It's okay if you have fears. This tutorial will help you identify the stories of your life, the ones you'd like to see in print. You may not know how to use a computer, but in the end it is an absolute necessity in preparing any manuscript for publication.

Publishers, agents or editors need your story presented in a Word or a PDF file. A PC (personal computer) usually comes with Microsoft Word, or it is available to download. An Apple computer comes with 'Pages' for word processing, and this can be converted to PDF. Or you can purchase Microsoft Word for MAC.

If this doesn't work for you, look for a friend or family member to enter your writing into a computer version for you. As for editing, these people may want to help, or you can hire a professional editor at between .01 to .02 cents per word.

Well, there you are. You can cling to your excuses, give up and let chunks of your story, your life, die with you, or you can (as they say these days) man-up, or lady-up, and get started...one chunk at a time and put the Me in Memoir now.

An Autobiography or a Memoir

You may ask: '*What is the difference between the two?*'

Not even bookstores or Amazon always get this correct. They arbitrarily lump them together in the same category or on the same shelf. Big mistake, because as you'll see below, there are differences.

A true Autobiography

_____ Literature genre, written by a person about their life story.

_____ Is written in chronological order.

_____ Narrates one's experience in life with its highs and lows from childhood to adulthood.

_____ Is generally written in first person POV, but third person can also be used.

_____ Is woven with intricate details of life events.

_____ Is popular with famous people and celebrities.

_____ Strives for factual and historical truths, and

can take much researching into records – both public and family.

A Memoir

_____ A Literary genre about real-life experience or experiences, taking place scattered throughout the writer's lifetime.

_____ Often intended as a message or lesson for the reader.

_____ A selection of events occurring anytime and anywhere during the writer's life.

_____ The word Memoir is taken from the French word Memoire, referring to reminiscence or remembrance.

_____ A specific segment or stage in one's life that proves to be pivotal, or a turning point.

_____ Either a single event, or a composite of events.

_____ Less formal than an autobiography.

_____ Written in either first or third person, but first person is more commonly accepted.

_____ Less fact checking and more delving into emotional truths, and family history.

Both are highly popular in today's market. Both require much brain searching, answer seeking, and tapping into long dormant memories.

"A memoir is not an autobiography. It's a true story told as a novel, using techniques of novelization. The author is allowed to compress events, combine

characters, change names, change the sequence of events, just as if he's writing a novel. But it's got to be true."
Homer Hickam

More fun quotes: Brainy Quotes Memoir

EXERCISE ONE:

Take about ten minutes and review the above choices, checking off the ones that best work for the presentation of your story. Make notes beside each if you wish.

How this book will help you put the ME in MEMOIR.

In looking through the contents, you may ask why we don't start writing until Lesson Six.

Not knowing where to begin is like setting out to reach a destination with no directions in mind. Lessons One through Five offer a road map, if you will, with preparation and insight into what you'll need on your journey.

Having an Academy Award story, combined with a great imagination, is one thing. You must learn the essential craft imperative in creating a profession manuscript. Otherwise, people (including family), will not enjoy reading it.

Like getting your ducks in a row, the lessons are designed to guide your progress, otherwise you will find yourself jumping back and forth in your files trying to rewrite, and cutting or pasting your scattered ducks back into line. In addition, you'll spend unnecessary time making changes and editing.

Lesson 1 – An Academy Award   The difference between an autobiography and a memoir.

Lesson 2 – Chunks for Your Story Choosing the part, or

parts of your life you want to include, and the use and importance of dialogue.

Lesson 3 – Setting, Place and Time

Lesson 4 – Point of View Choosing a point of view for yourself and your characters.

Lesson 5 – Character Development

Lesson 6 – Are we Ready to Begin Writing? Some do's and don'ts about Voice and Junk Words.

Lesson 7 – Hook, Pace, Action, Structure The hook or first one hundred words, Pace, Action, Structure.

Lesson 8 – Show v. Tell

Lesson 9 – It's a Wrap Conclusion, Denouement, Epilogue and types of endings.

Lesson 10 – The Dreaded Edit Stages and types of editing. Getting an editor. Editing reference sources.

Lesson 2 – Chunks for Your Story

Let's return to our mountain (autobiography) vs. chunk (memoir) theory. An autobiography is the entire mountain. Your memoir is made up of the chunks (your entire life) or a single chunk (a snippet) of rock that formed the mountain.

This is not to say you can't start taking notes early on in your life and build chronologically, much like journaling, but your purpose would be pulling out chunks to create the story and essence of a certain goal or a meaningful and inspirational event or events in your life. Your journal can lead to either an autobiography or memoir in the future.

A piece of advice...I'm retracing stories from my past and I regret not keeping journals. One event is the story of my son. When he was five-years old, he lost the ability to speak or understand speech. The diagnosis from the Neurological Pediatric team at UCLA concluded he had receptive and expressive aphasia brought on by unknown causes. An experimental medicine introduced at the time helped, but it took until he was in his teens to be 90% better.

Now, after so many years have passed, I've decided to write his story. This would be so much easier if I had kept records and written journals. Our memories can do two things...fail us, or allow us to distort events.

Lesson learned: It's never too late to start a new journal.

What about these chunks I spoke of earlier?

Single Chunk Example:

How I survived Breast Cancer.

Multiple Chunks (Simultaneous Chunks) Events

As a child I dreamed of being a dancer.

In school I loved gymnastics and I attended a dance school.

I studied Visual Arts in college and studied dance.

My first jobs were dancing with bands.

The big career opportunity came when I received a contract as a dancer with a Broadway stage play.

Single Chunks Scattered (Not Simultaneous)

Short stories made up of life events not necessarily related, but significant and inspiring to you and meaningful to the reader.

Each of these Chunks will automatically fall into their proper place, or location. These are a true part of your life, but there is no law saying you can't change the time and location.

This premise goes along with the idea you may want to keep real people anonymous, giving them a different name and location.

Maybe you have a friend or relation who prefers privacy. They could be offended if you include them in your book for all the world to see.

Unlike an autobiography, feel free to change your own identity to whatever degree you wish. This is especially true if it will make a difference later in avoiding unwanted attention or criticism.

EXERCISE TWO

For the next several minutes, pick the chunk or chunks you want to pursue, and write a note telling why.

For each Chunk or Chunks, give an approximate period of time these cover, such as:

Single Chunk – When I survived cancer from age forty to age forty-three, and the dates if you wish.

Chunks – Event one from age fourteen to age nineteen, Event two from age thirty to age thirty-six, etc.

How to Mine the Chunks

Maybe there is one huge or obvious event that

stands out in your life. It's a no-brainer. But what if there are a plethora of chunks throughout your life, each as interesting and exciting as the other?

Start by making a list. Do a little brain digging, and connecting of dots (or cells). Once you zoom in on a chunk, many roads will appear leading to it.

1. Visualize a large city. Got it? That's your Big Chunk (or the largest in this particular story). Give it a name and write it down.

2. Okay, not zoom in a little closer and notice the surrounding towns or communities. These are the satellite stories. Write these down, with short descriptions you can elaborate on later.

3. Zoom in more and see the roads and highways. How about a few houses and stores?

   Those are events that led up to and brought you to the Big Chunk. Write them down with a short description.

4. Use the Street View now and find people. These are the ones who you met along the way, travelled with you, influenced you, helped you, etc., to become part of the Big Chunk. These are your story characters. Identify them and write down tidbits or events they bring to your story.

EXERCISE THREE

Take some time to zoom in and out of your life chunks, writing them down, following the above suggestions with each step.

Once you get this outline completed and begin the story process, each of these will be elaborated on through vision, sense, smell, auditory, emotion, and feelings, as well as scene, location, time and year, weather, and yes, even dialogue.

This sounds daunting? Don't rush. Take one step at a time and your memory banks will do the rest of the work for you.

Use of dialogue

In the following example from *The Spaghetti Wars*, we have two scenes, one in downtown Boston, and the second at Rospo's Italian restaurant. But rather than telling about these places or the dilemma that Grae and Zoey face, as in the first selection, the details are divulged through dialogue.

How difficult is it to pen proper dialogue? Some will assert it's the trickiest part of writing. It is also one of the most important parts. Without it, your story is flat, dead. It's the key to Show v. Tell. (We'll learn more about this later).

Dialogue is what propels the story forward and allows your reader to be intimately familiar with your characters. In the world of writing fiction we find Plot Driven and Dialogue Driven manuscripts. Which do you think pulls a reader into the story?

Think about it, we engage in conversation daily, and we have internal speech (our voice). We know more about dialogue than we admit.

Let's share what we see in the following:

"I'm exhausted. I've had enough shopping-bag-therapy to last until next Black Friday," I said, struggling against the snow and wind.

"And we've got the packages to prove it," Zoey responded.

It was ten at night and the stores in downtown Boston were closing. Earlier, we walked to town from the restaurant, before the storm hit, not realizing how severe it would get.

With my head lowered against the onslaught, I began waving my hand in the air. "There has to be an empty taxi out here somewhere," I yelled to Zoey.

A Boston Checkered Cab pulled to the curb and the driver loaded our bags. "Where to, ladies?"

"Il Rospo Siciliano Restaurant, over on Hanover," I directed.

~ ~ ~

"Good evening Grae, Zoey, I see you women outdid yourselves. Let me give you a hand," Vincenzio, our head waiter offered, as we set our burgeoning shopping bags in a booth.

Although Rospo's was already closed for the night, a few of the regulars still nursed their booze of choice at the bar and watched ESPN. We stomped snow from our boots and hung our jackets in the coat room.

"Now what?" Zoey asked. "I'm not sure either of us should be driving home tonight. The roads are miserable."

"You've got a point. My nerves won't take plowing my car through this storm for over an hour," I said.

We wandered into the dim light of the dining room now filled with the ghosts of today's patrons, and I pulled aside one of the thick window drapes. We watched the wind carry crystal particles in drifts across the empty street.

"I love the scent of garlic, marinara sauce and wine mixed with smoke from the fireplace," I said. Zoey nodded.

My reverie was interrupted by Vincenzio.

"You ladies need a room?" he asked, pretending not to be eavesdropping.

"Um, no, I have a better idea." I grabbed Zoey's arm. "Let's go upstairs and see if Mama Rosa is still awake. She has a big sofa in her apartment. We'll camp out there tonight. It should be a hoot."

Do you see how the dialogue has led us to a new event, and left us curious about the outcome?

Why not write this same way? Like Vincenzio, we need to eavesdrop on our characters conversations.

Compare this to public speaking. Envision your readers to be a small group you stand before, ready to address. Have you prepared? Do you know your subject inside and out? If so, you'll feel confident, and your speech will come across natural, genuine and sincere. It will be real. But if you haven't prepared, your audience is going to feel uncomfortable, be put off, and walk out.

Be careful HOW they say it.

"Darling, those shoes are stunning," she *gushed*.

"What the hell is that?" he *exploded*.

If your sentence speaks to the reader with enough emotion and strength, you can skip the *gushing* and *exploding*. Stunning and hell are sufficient to make the point.

Some authors today have decided the word *'said'* is boring. To prove how clever (and amateurish) they are, they invent what editors and critics refer to as melodramatic dialogue or bookisms.

Here is my example:

"Danny, hurry the hell up, the cops will be here before we can disappear the body," Annie **growled** *in a hushed voice.*

"Don't go weirding out on me, Ann, I need you to get the lid off the damned box, and do it fast. I can't stand here all night holding up this jerk. Once we get him sealed in the crate, he'll be flying off on the next cargo plane," Danny **snapped***, glancing around the darkened warehouse, wishing Annie would move faster.*

"Who's the real jerk in this room, the living or the dead?" Annie blurted, "I mean, you've been acting like this is my fault. It wasn't me who stuck this guy in the freezer," she **mumbled***, grunting from*

the effort of prying at the box.

"No, but it is your fault that he showed up here in the first place. Annie, we gotta get out of here or we'll end up as cold and stiff as he is." Danny **spat** *the words at her, like she was an idiot.*

"This lid won't budge," she **whined***.*

Leaning forward, crowbar poised, she articulated her next words with the venom of a snake, "Here, lay the body on the floor and take this," she **hissed***.*

He dropped the body, grabbed the raised crowbar from Annie with one hand and slapped her out of the way with the other. "Fine, stupid," he chuckled. He gave her a menacing look and **snickered,** *"I'll get the box open, and then I'll deal with you."*

EXERCISE FOUR

Now read this dialogue once again, changing the bold words to 'said'. You'll see how the spoken words and the actions stay strong without the bookisms.

Rather than embellish a conversation, these bookisms often draw the reader away from the action or the tension of the moment.

Whenever you are tempted to toss in a bookism, ask yourself what words you can use to strengthen the dialogue itself. This doesn't mean you should never use an expression, or dialogue tag. Treat them like special delicacies, to be indulged in on occasion.

Allow your character to shout or whisper, but would they really thunder, splutter, snort or grunt their words? In certain situations they may plead, or giggle, especially when coupled with action.

As for punctuation, there's Cormack McCarthy, and then there's the rest of us. He uses few speech marks, apostrophes, colons, semi-colons and his sentences are clipped and sparse.

Take a look at his novel *The Road*. You'll find that his brilliance is found in verse that is crisp, fresh and precise.

Just let one of us take this style to an agent or publisher. It won't happen. We have to abide by the rules until the day comes we are worthy of casting our own style onto pages and eBooks.

Every line of dialogue should do three things.
1. Move the story forward
2. Disclose character
3. Sound realistic.

Keep it succinct, and don't let your people make chit-chatter or deliver long speeches. Use proper punctuation.

EXERCISE FIVE

Give dialogue a try. Take a few minutes, invent a couple of characters or use someone from your story, and have them start a conversation. Use proper punctuation, and follow the rules above.

To write dialogue is a powerful God-like phenomenon. You become the creator, molding your characters and breathing life into them as they converse with one another. It's a heady feeling.

Lesson 3 – Setting, Place and Time

Creating a vibrant sense of place and time is vital to bring your reader into the story with you.

The cast and characters of your story wait in the wings of the theater while you prepare a stage for them. You are the Set Director and it is *crucial* you provide your audience with a *cinematic* sense of place and time.

What do you visualize in your mind's eye? If this isn't clear to you, I recommend you consult with one of your characters, and take notes.

In *Listening to the Corn Grow*, the antagonist, Biggin Ray Bob Grady, took me by the hand and led me into Jubal's, the local watering hole where he spends too much of his time. He sat me down on an imaginary bar stool and went to join his buddies.

Leaning on the bar I observed the people, the surroundings and the action. I eavesdropped into muted or raucous conversations, listened to the clink of glasses and Patsy Cline sing from an old juke-box. I inhaled cigarette smoke flavored by the scent of wine and testosterone cologne. My shoes got stuck on the floor from spilled whiskey and puke, and I downed a cold one.

Later in the story, Ray Bob invited me to share his cell with him in the Nebraska State Penitentiary – and I did.

A classic example of a sense of place and time comes from writers like James Michener. His writing can be likened to the formation of a glacier or of a land. The plot often doesn't start until somewhere near the center of the book.

Tom Clancy is another author who shows us exactly where we are, but do we really need to know the number of bolts holding together a number ten hull panel of the USS *Theodore Roosevelt* nuclear-aircraft carrier?

Nuts and bolts aside, Clancy is a great inspiration. During an interview with Writer's Digest Magazine, *January 2001,* he advised aspiring writers to *"...just tell the damned story"*. Something to think about when you find yourself bogged down by overthinking, or during the editing process.

Today's readers value the opportunity to gain knowledge, and they invite limited amounts of information dumping. Let them in on descriptions that are new to them, such as horse racing, fly fishing, or shopping at Rodeo Drive in Beverly Hills. It's up to you to know what provides a vivid sense of place and time, or what threatens to collapse a scene on the spot. But don't trick your reader. Write true. You may be read by a fly fisherman.

Time is important. What year is it? What month? What is the weather like? Get your reader to feel the rain, or the warmth of the sunshine.

Place can be great fun. Dig deep into the surrounding land, the history, the people living there. There are no limits with Place. The action or event can be taking place on a jumbo jet, or a two seater Cessna. The ocean, river, cabin, city skyscraper, foreign land, and where you were when an event occurred.

Setting is Pivotal

Setting = Character = Plot   One leads to the other in the natural flow of the story.

In his novel *Wicked,* Gregory Maguire writes an amazing opening prologue where he describes:

"A mile above Oz, the Witch balanced on the wind's forward edge, as if she were a green fleck of the land itself, flung up and sent wheeling away by the turbulent air. White and purple summer thunderheads mounded around her. Below, the Yellow Brick Road looped back on itself, like a relaxed noose. Though winter storms and the crowbars of agitators had torn up the road, still it led, relentlessly, to the Emerald City. The Witch could see the companions trudging along, maneuvering around the buckled sections, skirting trenches, skipping when the way was clear. They seemed

oblivious of their fate. But it was not up to the Witch to enlighten them."

Here again we find in the first 113 words the elements conducive in welcoming the reader into the scene. (Read about the First One-Hundred Words later). Whenever I'm feeling at a loss for creating descriptive prose, I read these words for inspiration. He has set the scene and launched the story.

If that doesn't do it, read the opening to *Out of Africa*, by Isak Dinesen:

I had a farm in Africa, at the foot of the Ngong Hills. The Equator runs across these highlands, a hundred miles to the North, and the farm lay at the altitude of over six thousand feet. In the day-time you felt that you had got high up, near to the sun, but the early mornings and evenings were limpid and restful, and the nights were cold.

...it was Africa distilled up through six thousand feet, like the strong and refined essence of the continent. The colours were dry and burnt, like the colours in pottery.

...Nairobi was a motley place, with some fine new stone buildings, and whole quarters of old corrugated iron shops, offices and bungalows, laid out with long rows of Eucalyptus trees along the bare dusty streets.

Ms. Dinesen gives us a vivid sense of place that leads to character and plot (action). Be bold, and willing to dig into insignificant bits, like a macro image, zoom in and show.

Your Place or Mine?

When selecting a novel to read, I check the first few pages to see where and when it takes place, how well done is the setting and do I feel lured into the scene and location.

If your setting exists in the real world, take care with identifying information. The local natives will call you out if you get it wrong. A basic description will suffice, and then change up the names if you wish. Stores come and go, as do minor details, so create your own clever or whimsical names for streets and businesses. Add a cozy café, a street sign, a tree with a dog peeing on it, the deafening beat of the bass booming from a passing car. It's your imagination, driven by your muse.

People are shaped by their environment. Let the reader know where your characters live, work, and play, down to the private places in their life, such as the view from the porcelain throne.

EXERCISE SIX

With each chunk or pieces of chunks, write a scene

including the:

Setting:

Time:

Place:

Lesson 4 – Point of View

"How do I approach this task?"

Did you know you can do this the same way fiction is written with first Person past or present, or third person POV? It's a weighty task to stay within the point of view of the character who owns a scene. Ask yourself who is telling or experiencing the story? STAY in that Point of View throughout a scene. The following are brief lessons in POV.

First person POV

This is the most natural POV, since in our real world we view life from an "I" perspective. We're aware of first-person when a character uses **'I-me-my-mine'** in his or her speech.

In this POV you get to hear the thoughts of the character (you) and see the story through your eyes. The narrator (you) knows things the other characters don't.

The following sample is taken from my novel, *The*

Spaghetti Wars. This begins from Ruby Jean's POV, and in first person. Although we switch to action involving her mother Hanna, who is further away from where Ruby stands, we don't convert to her mother's POV. It is Ruby who sees the action, and relates what her mother says.

Steam billowed from a sludgy sidewalk grate in Boston's North End warming my legs.

"We're not at the library anymore, Nell," I said into my cell phone to my school friend. "It closed early. Now my mom says we can't sleep in the SUV because of this big storm. Be grateful you're not homeless." A cloud of frosty air muffled my words.

"Wait, I gotta go, my mother's calling me."

I peered around the corner of a four-story red brick building on Hanover Street. At the far corner of the building a green neon sign read: il Rospo Siciliano Ristorante.

"Ruby Jean, can you hear me? Come down here," Mother called to me from the dark alleyway that burrowed between the restaurant and a retail store.

A fast-moving truck sent gray slush across the sidewalk and I ducked into the alley to avoid getting wet, but my shoes and feet were already soaked.

"Mom, we can sleep in the car. I like it

there."

Mom's head stuck out from a basement window about five feet below the sidewalk and she was wearing her Mary Poppins like hat — so not cool.

"No, this is better, and safer. We're supposed to get a ton of snow tonight. Help me climb out of this window and we'll move our bedding inside."

I reluctantly left the precious warmth of the steam and leaned over to grab the outstretched hand of my mom, Hanna Argolin Richardson.

Together we pulled blankets and pillows from the red SUV and dumped them into the basement of what looked to be a large Italian restaurant. Then we drove to an asphalt pocked parking lot promising to be free from 9 p.m. to 5 a.m., and walked back to our new digs. Once inside, Mom closed the window. It went down with a loud thump, and we held our breath. There was the sound of distant footsteps from the floor above, but nothing more.

Mom stacked blankets in layers on the cement floor for protection against the cold, and I found my sleeping bag and spread it out.

"This is not so terrible. We'll get through it, I promise," Mom said with a *tinge of doubt in her voice.*

"Mom, we lived in a beautiful home with everything we needed. Dad made a ton of money, and we were fine. Now look at us, breaking into a restaurant basement...and you think this is 'not terrible?'"

"Don't be disrespectful. I'm not the reason we're here."

"No, you're not. I'm sorry." We hugged and curled up in our sleeping bags.

I smelled spaghetti sauce — my tummy growled.

Take a minute and reread this. Identify the following:

1. Who is the narrator of this opening scene?
2. What did she reveal to be the location?
3. What other information did she reveal?
4. Did the writer set up a hook to capture the reader's interest?

When you write, you may find you are in a character's head, immersed in a scene, then slip unaware from one POV, or tense, to another. It's important to get the writing side of your brain to understand this is not allowed. It is mandatory that you know who's POV you are in. It is incumbent on you to keep this focus.

Advantage of First-person POV

It is subjective.

The reader always knows who is seeing the action.

You can choose a voice more freely.

In first-person you may use slang, bad grammar, etc., while third-person restricts you to standard English.

First-person allows free access to what the person is thinking.

Things to overcome in First-Person or First-Person Present

Dialogue may be difficult to incorporate because the narrator must be in the scene.

We can't see the person, because they can't see themselves. But they can know how they look, or glimpse themselves in a reflection.

In first-person we must stay within this persons parameters. For example, your character has no knowledge of what is happening off scene, other than through telephone, television, internet, or someone telling them first hand.

A way to change this is by switching POV in a new chapter or scene, but this can confuse your reader if not handled with discretion. The use of 'rabbits' * * * works to signify a change in scene.

EXAMPLE: This is taken from the sequel to **The Spaghetti Wars**.

Unravioli is written a little different, in first person PRESENT. We are in the present action now. Either of these are perfect for writing your memoir, although first person past is a tad easier.

Unlike me, there are people who hop out of bed in the morning with purposeful and seamless lives. The one-thousand Egyptian cotton thread-count sheets on my bed are smooth and uncomplicated. This is the type of life I wish for.

Detective Ron Randic, the downtown dick, phoned me at six this morning to tell me my ex-husband was found gut shot and left to die in a parking lot beneath a Boston bridge. I didn't kill him – though I did try once during a heated argument.

My vivid imagination conjures up the scene. Martin is gasping his last breath, cursing, while someone stands over him with a smoking gun. In my fantasy I am straining to see if the killer has polished red nails, or a metro sexual manicure.

Slipping my favorite nightgown to the floor, I gaze at my long legs, thin waist and flat chest. At least my butt doesn't drag, and my boobs don't droop. These tits will never see the floor. My closest friend, Zoey Osmond, complained to me recently. "Grae," she said, "be thankful you have little boobs. These hooters can see every step I take. Even the bodacious brassieres I purchase, at no small cost I might add, won't tilt them to high-beam.

These are the opening paragraphs and scene. Let's

break it down a little while we're here.

1. What is the hook, or event that attracts the reader's attention?
2. Where are the locations?
3. What is the narrators name?
4. What does she reveal about herself and her physical features?
5. Did you imagine yourself in the scene with her?

When can we switch POV?

As you read above, switch at the completion of a scene, but it's best to let the reader know by adding a signal, such as 'rabbits'.

And you may change POV at the completion of a chapter or section, such as Part 1.

Third-person POV

This is when we, the creator, writes "he" "she" or "they", rather than "I". This POV requires further choices. You get to choose between:

Third-person Omniscient Where we know everything about every one of our characters, including the places and the events placed in our scenes. This is sometimes referred to as the "God's eye" view.

The fun part with this point of view comes from the ability to observe from many angles, similar to a camera.

Now that I've given you these options, I recommend keeping it simple.

My POV? I like First Person Present or Past.

EXERCISE SEVEN

Which POV do you choose to write your story in? Try writing a few sentences in the role of the narrator, and include dialogue.

Lesson 5 – Character Development

Get familiar with your characters before you introduce them to your reader. Will you be interacting with Aunt Allison? You already know many things about her, but refresh your memory by making a list. This will include facets of her personality, a description of her appearance, and a brief summary of her place in your life. You know and love (or not) Aunt Allison.

It's important in your analysis above to add qualities that go beyond general description. For example, you might want to add the quirky wart on her nose, and how this intrigued you as a child. Or you could include the way she punished your cousins by using a switch on their behinds and how you felt. In the writing world this is called 'Fleshing out your character'.

This gives your reader the feeling they know your characters inside and out.

You're painting a visual picture of each of your characters. And don't forget the other senses. Do you remember the smell of Aunt Allison's perfume? Was her home always filled with smoke from Uncle Al's cigars or cigarettes? How did it feel to tramp through the snow with your cousins?

Another analysis to help reveal more about your characters can include some of the following:

o Date and place of birth
o Childhood history
o Schools, degrees, skills
o Level of Intelligence
o Work history
o Parents and siblings
o Mate and children
o Present location and occupation
o Political affiliations
o Major accomplishments
o Talent, humor
o Difficult issues during life (divorce, surgery, etc.)
o Any infirmities and disabilities, general health
o Flaws, habits and anything unique
o Mannerisms, body type, body language
o Friends, peers
o Moral and ethical values
o Preferences
o Goals, motivations, dreams
o Nervous mannerisms or weird habits

EXERCISE EIGHT

With this exercise you have your character write an imaginary letter to you. Getting into their head can take you back in time and help you recall specific or incidental events.

When including them in your story, draw on their passions, thrills or fears. Ask yourself if this character is three-dimensional, multi-faceted, and multi-layered. They need to have clear identities, be unique, and believable.

They must be complex and possess conflicting traits. It's possible for a person to be frivolous but responsible; slovenly yet dependable; loving yet daring. A flat character is shallow and always predictable. They become stereotypes, like the shifty-eyed thief and the anorexic model. What do they most fear? What is their motivation in overcoming obstacles?

A Name paints a thousand pictures

If you've chosen to change the names of your characters from real-life to fictional, look online for lists of names — male, female, last names, by country of origin, and more. Choose a tough name for a street fighter, a classy name for a female reporter, a weak name for a coward or a scandalous name for a scoundrel. In my novel *Listening to the Corn Grow*, I chose the name, Biggin Ray Bob Grady as the antagonist. He is identified and defined by his personality, how he dresses, his tastes in women, food, etc.

The name must fit the person. John, Joe, Sue are NOT memorable by name alone. That's not to say they can't be incredible in their roles, but it helps to label them well. Avoid names beginning with the same first letter, such as Betty, Barb, Beatrice and Bella, in the same scene.

When someone with a name appears in our story, it should conjure up an image in your reader's mind. What is your first impression when you hear these names?

- o Ted Dishman
- o Zoey Osmond
- o Martin Notorangeli
- o Alexander Richardson
- o Dorrington Mud

Think about the names we'll never forget, and how they create an immediate response when we hear them:

- o Scarlett and Rhett
- o Zorro
- o James Bond
- o Tom Brady
- o Adolph Hitler
- o Shrek
- o Winston Churchill
- o Madonna

Again, allow your characters to bring the five senses into your story.

From *Listening to the Corn Grow*:

"She takes Mattie's fingers between her lips and runs her tongue over the tips, tasting remnants of banana pudding, and watches him as he giggles with delight."

You get to be responsible for conveying these sensory experiences to your reader. You want them to taste the pudding, feel the pain, hear the wind.

Listen to your Characters: They will whisper secrets in your ear and flaunt who they are.

"Every human being has hundreds of separate people living under his skin. The talent of the writer is his ability to give them their separate names, identities, personalities, and have them relate to other characters living with him." *Mel Brooks*

EXERCISE NINE

List at least two of your characters along with as many of the above characteristics befitting each one.

Lesson 6 – Are we Ready to Write?

"Start writing, no matter what. The water does not flow until the faucet is turned on."

Louis L'Amour

Oh right, back to those dreaded words – **'Where and how do I begin?'**

The big picture and the monumental jolt of emotions attached to this can and will get your head spinning. My advice is to find the closest beginning point in your story, or chunk. A date can help. Now put yourself back there. Shut your eyes, take a cleansing breath, and let your memory take you to the event.

Pretend you are revealing this story or event to someone dear to you. This helps your story become real and intimate.

Once you feel ready, start writing from your heart. Don't spare words. Elaborate. Use senses – cold, hot and odors. Visualizations, whenever possible, will take the person you are showing with you on this journey. Many of our experiences happen when we are alone. You are not alone now, you have your confidant with you. Picture a best friend, or make up your new imaginary best friend.

Don't worry about getting anyone's attention, or coming up with a clever hook while in this stage of the process. It will come later. The important thing now is to start taking us with you along that road to your journey.

EXERCISE TEN

Spend a minimum of 30 minutes and begin a chunk of your story.

Dialogue and Voice

What is Voice?

How do we define the mystery of voice in fiction? Voice is a puzzling term to new writers. Simply said, voice comes from inside your head and onto the pages you write. It's the little voice in you, and it sounds like you, and will come across this way in the story.

In fiction you'll have the voice of the narrator (you) and the voices of your characters (others you include). The better you know your characters, the better you'll hear their voices.

For example: How does Uncle Bill sound when he talks in his nasal raspy voice?

With dialogue, we want it to be relevant to the

overall story and where it is going. In other words, don't let Uncle Bill take the reader down some other path with his own stories, unless these enhance your own event or adventure.

For example, you say:

I remember Uncle Bill and the days my brothers and I spent with him on the farm. He was a wizened old coot, always had a cigarette between his lips, and he would spit often. Once we played in the hay loft and my brother Joel got his foot stuck between the floor boards.

Uncle Bill loved to tell this story to his cronies. It went like this...

"Those young kids was up thar playing as usual, diving in and out of dat hay and scaring up the mice and stray barn kittens...an Joey, well he goes and breaks his dang foot."

Here you have Uncle Bill elaborating on your story with his own version, in his voice and POV. It's up to you if you want Bill to intrude further, or not.

Some Do's and Don'ts to think about with Voice:

DO use active rather than passive verbs ("Emmy dropped...or drops...the glass" is active; "the glass was dropped" is passive)

DON'T use awkward verbs (have, appeared, exist)

Avoid weak, inert verbs (The scent of rotten fish was making him sick. The scent of rotting fish made me feel sick.)

DO use potent, present, active verbs. (run/chase, hit/strike, complain/bitch)

DO use slang, local dialect or accents discreetly. If your character is from Louisiana—or any locale that has a distinct sound—it's okay to include this in early conversation, but play it down as you progress.

JARGON and DIALECT will keep the character unique, but can detract from the potency of the dialogue or narrative.

How do you know if you're writing in a skillful voice? Try reading your work out loud. Awkward and stilted words will beg to be rewritten.

Ya'll and *reckon* do not a Southerner make. You need to search the elements of the dialect, grammar, syntax and word choice to make it authentic. Break the mold. It's okay to use misspelled words, as in the above sample with Uncle Bill.

JUNK Words

Starting your story means examining a few common writing errors. One of these is how to AVOID Junk Words by strengthening your verbs and nouns. <u>An exception to this can be found in dialogue.</u>

o About

o Almost

- Already
- Am
- Appear
- Approximately
- Are
- As
- Basically
- Been
- Being
- Close to
- Even
- Eventually
- Exactly
- Exist
- Finally
- Has
- Have
- Here
- Kind of
- ly words
- Nearly
- Now
- Practically
- Really
- Seems
- Simply
- Somehow

- o Somewhat
- o Sort of
- o Suddenly
- o That
- o Then
- o Truly
- o Utterly
- o Very
- o Was
- o Were

Here is another example: Did you know THAT THAT word on THAT list could be replaced?

...ING endings tend to make a sentence weak.

Avoid repeating words in close proximity. Use your thesaurus to replace words, rather than repeat them. The sound of repetition will stand out when you read, or read out

loud.

Here is an example from Norman Mailer's *The Naked and the Dead*:

Ridges laid down his shovel and looked at him. His face was patient but there was some concern in it.

"What you trying to do, Stanley?" he asked.

"You don't like it?" Stanley sneered.

"No, sir, Ah don't."

"Aah, fug it," he said, turning away.

Mailer said the use of obscenities was

unfashionable during that period, therefore, changing the spelling helped. Again, it's not necessary to make every sentence sound local, but you can toss in a word or two occasionally to keep the person in character, and to hear his voice.

Body language is another aspect of Voice. Expressions like; lowered his eyes, cocked her head to one side, licked her lips, bounded along, etc., can flesh out the character's personality through their conversation and add visual depth.

We'll cover more writing tips as we go.

EXERCISE ELEVEN

Let's go back and see how your story writing is progressing. How many paragraphs did you get done? Did you build the basis for that first chunk? Great.

Now take time to search for your voice based on the above. Then check what you've written to search out Junk Words, etc.

Lesson 7 – Hook, Pace, Action, Structure

The First One Hundred Words

Now let's take a look at a subject I love...Your First One-Hundred Words. This is where you drill down your opening to just that, and peak the readers interest.

"Mama, are you a virgin?"

These words open the novel, *Coffee Will Make You Black,* by April Sinclair. April was part of a panel at a conference I attended a few years back, and these five words resonated with me. They represent the quintessential first words of a novel. What do these five words convey to us, the reader?

The speaker is young and less educated and likely a female who is bold and inquisitive.

The opening scene continues...

"I was practicing the question in my head as I set the plates with the faded roosters down on the shiny

yellow table. When Mama came back into the kitchen to stir the rice or turn the fish sticks or check on the greens, I would ask her.

This afternoon at school a boy named Michael had passed me a note with "Stevie" written on it; inside it had asked if I was a virgin."

This is how to get your readers attention!

EXERCISE TWELVE

Write a few notes about what these sentences revealed. What did you learn?

By following a dynamic set of key elements at the outset of your story, you'll entice a reader/shopper to reach for their credit card and buy your book.

How many times have you opened a book and perused just the first few paragraphs? Maybe on Amazon.com, or another online bookstore, you have clicked: "Look Inside" to view these pages before you purchased? Maybe you're seeking a book with sixteenth century London as a setting, or New York City during the sixties.

Give your potential reader the information they want, and be specific. Here is another example:

Dana Coulter left the imposing building of the 9th Precinct Police complex in downtown Philadelphia. Her anger heightened at the sight of snarled rush *hour traffic inching along Cedar. She brushed her auburn hair out of her eyes and fumbled with her umbrella, ready to face the freezing November rain. A voice from behind startled her—she knew who it was and anticipated the large filthy gloved hand even before it wrapped across her cheek and lips. With an insane rush of adrenaline, and without an ounce of remorse, she spun around and drove the four-inch tip of the umbrella into the groin of Hardy Bono. Then she hailed a taxi.*

With these first 112 words, what do we learn?

___ Location: We are outside of a police precinct in Philadelphia.

___ About the narrator: Name, sex and hair color.

___ The time of day, month and the weather conditions.

___ Her mood.

___ We immediately learn about her personality through her response and actions.

___ The name of the antagonist.

___ The story is sure to be fast-paced.

___ The hook has been set.

Your first 100 words must catch your reader's attention and make them salivate for more.

Here is a great example from the opening of Tom Grundner's *Midshipman Prince*:

Lucas Walker did not want to open his eyes. He did not even want to continue living, but that was irrelevant. He knew he had to do both.

His world was pitching wildly. From his position, flat on his back in his cabin, it was as if he was motionless and the planet itself had gone insane. The timbers of the old merchantman, normally softly groaning, had been shrieking in agony for the past twelve hours. This had done nothing for Walker's head, which felt like it would explode any minute.

We know:

___ The Narrator's name and his mood.
___ The setting is aboard a merchant ship at sea.
___ It's a wooden ship, undoubtedly a sailing vessel.
___ They are in trouble, probably in a storm.
___ Walker is not feeling well, either hung-over or seasick.

In 91 words the hook is set. There is no way you're going to stop reading.

How do your first 100 words measure up? They already can be found in the words you have written thus far.

Now you need to dump unnecessary words or sentences, and tighten it up.

Pace

Stories differ in pace. A history will move at a

slower meter. Action revs up to non-stop, however, the pace needs to be balanced. If you include fast paced action, take time out to breathe during a quiet night of romance, a funeral, or sleep. I call it taking time to smell the roses. Find the rhythm and the beat of your story and keep the pace in check.

Have you left the reader hanging from a cliff by his pinky finger? The essence of pace is to escalate or lower the speed, hang them by their fingernails — then STOP. This automatically catapults the story forward. Every scene builds toward the final scene at the conclusion of the story. Your pace *must* move the action and the reader forward and culminate just in time. Know when to say *The End*.

Action

Like we brought out earlier, before there can be dialogue and interaction between your characters, you must set up, or at least be aware of, the scene and structure where the action takes place. Your reader gets settled in and becomes a spectator in your theater. Focus more on the *where* than the *how*.

Much like pace, action requires attention to highs and lows, pulling your reader along, then letting them take a breather. Non-stop action will exhaust both you and your reader.

Structure

Each of your small chunks, or the big chunk, needs to follow this basic structure. One time through may work for the big chunk, and the same for each of your small chunks, or short anecdotes.

- **Place**   A room, office, hospital, police station...briefly identifies the opening words of your scene, by either narrative or through the eyes and dialogue of your character. As the story continues, you add more depth and texture to the place.
- **Time**   Season, month, day, hour, holiday...are immediately shown in the opening.
- **Why**   The event...what brought these people or this person to the scene.
- **Action**   Movement, dialogue, interaction...the scene being played out.
- **Crisis**   Rather than the entire scope of your premise and inciting incident that the story chunk is based on, this is specific to this single scene. It is a lessor incident.
- **Culmination** Each scene has a high point. This is the mini-hook that carries the reader to the next scene. (or chapter)
- **Resolution**   Also part of our cyclical analogy, and can be a partial resolution. A small problem gets solved, but another comes into play.
- **Catalyst**Leads to the next event, if there is one.

At the conclusion of a scene, we want the reader to think about what has transpired and look forward to what comes next.

Note to self...*I must continue to throw in obstacles and relive problems, overlapping hurdles...and the more the better. You, the narrator, and some of your* *major characters, must work at getting through this adventure alive, and maybe save the world as well.*

"I have no influence over them. (characters) I'm only an observer, recording. The story is always being told by the characters themselves." *Erskine Caldwell*

EXERCISE THIRTEEN

Let's rework what you've accomplished so far. Based on the information we've covered, how do you grade your first 100 words?

What about your pace, action and structure?

Does a scene end with a catalyst?

Lesson 8 – Show v. Tell

"Don't tell me the moon is shining; show me the glint of light on the broken glass."

Anton Chekhov

Other than POV (Point of View), this is the thorniest lesson for new writers to grasp. Here are the words found in the opening paragraphs of *Miranda of Luckenbach*, a short story, and an example of how we can show through narrative as well as dialogue.

This is telling:

Luckenbach is in the southeastern county of Gillespie Texas, has a population of three, and a permanent ghost. Me. My name is Miranda, and I'm a ghost living in a ghost town. A narrow dust-pocked road turns at a sharp angle where I sit combing my hair. Many men were hung from the hanging tree at the entrance to town, but I was purposely drowned.

This is Showing:

I sit in the arms of a water-smoothed tree limb that belongs to a handsome tree, and fiddle with a three foot twine of my matted hair. It's lost the luster of the old days. They say when we die our hair keeps right on growing. My hair keeps growing and I've been dead for nearly ten years.

I'm Miranda Kincaid, and I live, or is it lived, in Luckenbach, Texas. No joke — I'm a ghost, living in a ghost town.

Damn, this mess just won't untangle! Back when I was young and beautiful my hair would shine a fiery red and I'd toss it in the breeze and flirt with Byron. Now it resembles the dull copper of the bell hanging on the door of the General Store, 'cept that bell's got more green on it. My hair ain't that green yet, but the neighbor's wife, who died two years ago, her hair has gone kind of like a gooey pile of wet cement.

Luckenbach, population 3 living souls, an assortment of chickens, and one permanent ghost — me, lies hidden beneath a full moon just thirteen miles from Fredericksburg in southeastern Gillespie County, Texas.

Giving up on my hair, I scoot further out on the limb and dangle my feet in the creek.

Byron loved my hair; among other things. One day we got naked and hid in a field of bluebonnets. We kissed and played. He picked a handful of wild flowers, showered them across my bare belly, sucked a dandelion from my navel and ate it. "...You and me and dandelion wine..." he sang.

I had some once...dandelion wine. It got my head spinning. Byron's kisses had that same effect.

Laws of Show and Tell

__ Telling is shallow and boring.

__ Showing takes the reader inside of the story, from one-dimensional to three dimensional.

__ Showing reveals motives and intention.

__ Showing connects the reader through the senses.

__ Showing reveals the voice and dialogue of the characters.

__ Showing gives the reader a sense of time and place, especially if the story is set in an unfamiliar place or time.

__ Showing deepens the suspense.

__ Showing helps the reader to understand relationships.

__ Showing heightens expectations of what comes next.

__ Showing makes the story real for the reader.

__ Never use an adjective or adverb unless it is necessary. This will strengthen your sentences and allow you to show rather than tell.

__ Don't over-describe. Write clear, succinct sentences to create a clearer picture.

___ Don't over-dramatize a scene. It's one thing if your character is a drama queen, but don't take it to the point of melodrama.

Have you ever listened to someone tell you a story, going on and on and on to the point of utter boredom? It goes something like:

My daughter and her husband are coming to visit me at the lake. I have a new grandson. I wish my husband, Al Senior, were still alive. I don't want my daughter to know I've been tested for cancer. Then I held my grandson Andrew. He has dimples and intelligent eyes. I didn't know my daughter has cancer, too.

Not getting the feeling?

First of all, let me **TELL** you, this is known as **TELLING the story**. You are **telling** me about these people I don't know.

Now let me **SHOW** you how to draw your reader into the above story, the scene, the climate, the scents and sounds.

"It is one of those glorious summer days at the lake when the mosquitos are off hiding beneath shade bushes and bees are droning near fragrant roses. I can't decide what to wear.

My daughter Lizbeth, and her husband Don, are on their way to visit me. I'll be meeting my new three week old grandson!

Oh, I'd love to jump into the water from the dock and cool down like I know Liz and Don will do...but just look at these wrinkles! I pull on my standard cotton shirt with the roll-up sleeves.

I fiddle with the V-neck to make sure I do a good job of hiding the bandages from where they took the biopsy. Then I pull on denim capris.

I feel sad, but this isn't the time to talk about morose subjects. Rather, it's a time of joy, to celebrate meeting my new grandson. I slip into thongs, and tuck my blonde/gray curls into a straw hat.

I fuss for a few minutes with the gift I made for Andrew (I wanted to call him Andy, but was scolded for that). A car pulls into the drive of our summer cabin.

Where is Al? He should be hear for this moment, to hold his first grandson, see the sweet dimples and smiles. 'Oh Al, why did you leave me? These are supposed to be our golden years together.'

Never mind. I'm here. I'll enjoy this for both of us.

"There you are, darlings, come in, come in."

After our hugs and kisses, Don sets a very large baby carrier on the sofa. Nestled deep within is a wee baby.

"Would you like to hold him, Mom?"

"Of course I would. I must count his dimples and look into his intelligent eyes."

It is then I notice a patch bandage much like mine on her lower neck.

Now we've covered a few of the choices you need to make before you start clicking away at the keyboard (or on that yellow legal pad).

EXERCISE FOURTEEN

Take a few minutes and add your observations from above:

What is the Chunk or Chunks

Location

Time frame

Descriptions

People

Motivating or inspiring points

Point of View

Why choose Showing over Telling

Now read your writing thus far and rate yourself on Show v. Tell. Name some ways you can change this.

"The plot and characters dance a sinister tango, entangling and weaving themselves into a story. And then the details come raining down."

Jaqueline Girdner

Lesson 9 – It's a Wrap

Denouement, Conclusion, Epilogue

Otherwise known as Resolution. This is where we get together with our characters and solve the problems presented throughout the action, crises, and culmination.

Will a heroine save the day and how? Who lives, and who dies? Who laughs, and who cries?

The cyclical mini-resolution that we've positioned at the end of scenes, or chapters, now comes together in a culmination.

We covered some of this in Structure. Here's a way to view it like a roller coaster ride.

We have:

The inciting incident = The rising action as the story opens.

Conflicts = The ups and downs of the story.

The lesser resolution = Resolves one problem, but not the overall conflicts.

The lesser conflicts = Further developments in

your story.

The crises = We hang for a moment or a period, poised and ready.

The culmination, conclusion, final resolution, denouement = The story dips and coasts to a stop.

Until the end comes, you need to keep your readers on the edge, wanting to know what comes next. This won't work if you've given out too much prior information through action, dialogue and character. Otherwise, the resolution will be redundant.

A realistic conclusion can be accomplished in several ways:

_____1. Through the natural process of dialogue and action as our characters overcome the climactic obstacles they face. This could take several scenes or chapters.

_____2. A mixture of narrative, dialogue and action can take your reader through the conflict and resolution.

_____3. In a story written in first person, the speaker is the one who generally divulges the resolution as we follow their life.

_____4. Omniscient narrative is appropriate in some instances – when everyone else in the scene is dead or gone.

The Wrap

This is a commonly known movie term that sheds information and perspective on what has taken place, or a wrap-up. This is what a denouement consists of –

putting the pieces of your story together and coming to a clear conclusion.

The Epilogue

A story may conclude with a harrowing rescue scene. We've learned who survived and who didn't make it, and we know how they were rescued. The crises and conclusion are complete and the scene ends with yourself and your characters standing dripping wet on a deserted beach. Do you, the author, leave them shivering in the cold? With the epilogue, you have the opportunity to tie up the loose ends. What happened when you returned home? How did the adventure affect your future? It's common to make a gap in time from when the action stopped, to the epilogue. This can be days, months or years.

What do you want your readers to take away? How do they feel? Happy? Sad? Moved? Inspired? The conclusion, or epilogue, gives you the opportunity to instill this in your readers. It's simple. They'll remember five things; the hook, a vivid sense of place and time, your unique characters, the plot and the conclusion. But...will they?

The Circular Ending

Endings give an answer to the earliest questions posed, as far back as the initial hook. They tie together the questions and answers. A circular ending uses an early paragraph where a premise or question is posed and is repeated at, or near, the end.

Matching v. Non-matching Ending

Similar to a circular ending, a matching ending answers the original premise. A non-matching ending involves a different set of characters. The original people have been replaced perhaps due to length of time, or death. We see this take place in a saga.

Surprise Ending

The O'Henry ending. For example, we might be duped by a red-herring – something or someone placed in the story to throw the reader off track. In "Who-done-its", everything possible is done to mislead the reader. Drop subtle hints, but never divulge enough information to allow them to solve the mystery until its time.

Trick Ending

The resolution and final actions will let us believe the story is over. Bam! It turns out there's more to it than we perceived.

Summary Ending

This is where you use narrative to TELL your audience the ending. Tom Wolfe successfully uses a summary ending for *The Bonfire of the Vanities*. Would you rather show your readers the end through scene and dialogue?

Open Ending

Allows your readers to come to their own conclusion as to how things turned out for you and your characters. Here is an example of an open ending:

A Gunfight, a western movie set in a Mexico border town where Johnny Cash and Kirk Douglas live. They are retired gunfighters who are goaded by the townsfolk into a duel or final shoot-out.

Douglas's wife is appalled by the idea. Cash's girlfriend is scared.

The entire community gathers at a local bullfight arena dressed in their Sunday best. In a holiday mood, they pass the alcohol and place bets on the outcome of the altercation.

An announcer introduces Cash and Douglas as they stride to the center of the arena. The crowd is hushed with anticipation. A bell tolls the hour – the signal to draw.

Shots ring out and we see Douglas fall to the ground. The camera pans the faces of the shocked crowd as they realize what they've done. The story concludes with his wife and son, and the grief they suffer.

Aha...but that's not the end of the film. There's a flashback, and this time we see Cash fall to the ground, followed by the same pan of faces in the shocked crowd. Saddened by her loss, his girlfriend prepares to leave town. On the street she sees Douglas with his happy family. The two women lock eyes in mutual understanding.

Who really died? The audience makes the choice – it's an open ending.

Ending with a beginning

...to be continued. One story reaches a conclusion but is catapulted forward with a new hook to await a resolution in the next book, sequel, or movie.

Choose with care how you resolve and conclude your story. The reader will remember the inspiration, fear, love, hate, passion, adventure – forever.

EXERCISE FIFTEEN

How do you foresee your story concluding? Take a few minutes and try playing with an ending.

Lesson 10 – The Dreaded Edit

The Elements of Editing

First Read – On the Go

One way to edit and rewrite is to make changes as you go. If you are interrupted, leave your story for several hours or days, come back and read what you previously wrote. This helps lead you into your next scene or chapter.

This can be in its entirety or select the last few pages or paragraphs. By doing this, you are accomplishing your first edit, or first read. Another good exercise is to return to your work and read it out loud. This will give you a fresh acoustic view of the changes needed and give you confidence in your writing.

Second Read – Content

When your story is complete, put it away for no less than two weeks. Two months is better. Send your characters on a vacation and put the story out of your mind. Don't allow them to return until you are ready.

Ready means that you have the time to devote to a

complete and thorough re-read. This time you go from page one to the end without stopping. A good way to do this is to print it. (This provides another backup to your electronic file).

During this read, limit your markup to a check mark reference next to the sentence, to be revised later. This read is for you to get an overall sense of the complete book.

HINT - To own it, print a second copy, place it in a box or a manila envelope and mail it to yourself. Don't open it. The postmark and the fact that it is sealed, proves it is your work. This is a secondary legal copyright.

Third Read – Revisions

Best done with your computer copy, this is where you flesh out your characters, see how your dialogue resonates, fill in your scenes and setting. Revisions can go from a single word to entire paragraphs and chapters. If your timeline is off, use your cut and paste features to take scenes to a new area of the book. Revisions are slow and tedious, but try to look at it as filling in the blanks, and letting your people take time to smell the roses.

You need this experience to dwell with your characters on a very personal level. Sit down with one of them and have a conversation. Ask them if there is anything else they want to add to the story to help make them real in your readers mind. Get into each character's head, walk the walk, and build as you go.

An interesting exercise is to write down the number

of words in your manuscript before you begin your revision. Some say revising shortens your word count while you tighten the sentences, and make your paragraphs succinct and defined. Or, the word count will increase as you add insight and depth into your characters and their environment.

Fourth Read – Line or Copy Edit

My choice is to once again print the entire manuscript. A unique phenomenon occurs when editing using the computer screen versus the printed page. I have no scientific explanation, but our eyes miss many many errors on the screen. Try comparing, you'll see what I mean.

Things like poor word choice, stiff dialogue, or awkward writing is corrected now. Minor flaws can be fixed with a word change or two. Punctuation, spelling and grammar are corrected.

Peer through a magnifying glass at every word, sentence and nuance to weed out errors. 'Select – All' and run it through 'Spell Check'. Take each of the 'JUNK words' and run them through, finding ways to replace them.

Look at your margins, indents and the overall layout. When an agent or publisher sees your work for the first time, they expect – demand – it be perfect.

Gone are the days when you could submit '*A Good Story*' and have the publishers ecstatic to the point of requesting it on content alone...handing it to their editors to solve your problems and errors for you. Why? They don't have to. They receive too many submissions daily, solicited or otherwise...print perfect.

Okay, this is the time to grade your work. Here are the elements you need to check. Make a copy of this list and paste it on your forehead from the minute you write your first word to the last punctuation mark of your work. These are essential in writing and editing fiction:

1. Is your setting crisp, cinematic and full?

2. Is your character fleshed out, rounded, real? Believable?

3. Does your dialogue carry the story, or are you, as the narrator, telling rather than showing?

4. Do you take unnecessary time with narrative and telling?

5. Have you stayed in Point of View within each scene and chapter?

6. Do you catapult each scene and chapter ahead with a resolution and a new captivating hook?

7. Keep alert for disjointed actions or thoughts that will jolt your reader away from the story.

8. Does your story lag, include unnecessary phrases, or take the reader away from the theme?

9. Is your dialogue stilted or awkward?

10. Have you thoroughly researched your subjects and places for accuracy?

11. Is the pace congruent with the action and plot?

12. Do you avoid word repeats in close proximity?

13. Are your verbs active rather than passive?

14. Do you avoid -ly words, adjectives, adverbs?

15. Did you clip your clichés?

At this point, you'll agree writing is a lonely art. Friends and family will praise you for your efforts, but don't expect them to become involved. Yes, they'll ask to read it, but that's them being patronizing or curious. Or they want to see what you've written about them!

When to let a friend or family member read your story.

Is this person going to be forthright and honest, or

are they the type to praise for the sake of building your ego?

Do your friends/family know things about your subject/plot that can contribute to the overall story? If they do, this is a big plus.

Get a professional proofreader or editor.

This is great if you can afford it and if you chose the right person or company. Caution is advised. Some will claim to know the business, but still you should ask for references and credentials. Otherwise you're wasting time and money, and worse, you may take their advice – and it's wrong!

Join a workshop or critique group.

As the founder and leader of these animals, I can say a good critique group can be invaluable. But...a bad group can ruin you and your writing. There are critique group horror stories. They don't call them 'Read and Bleed' sessions for nothing. Jealousy, ignorance, lack of tact, wrong information, callousness, and plain stupidity, can't be allowed. You will know a reputable group if they offer guidelines, have a facilitator vs. a free-for-all, and stick to the rules of critique etiquette.

This is a great place to read your work out-loud. Or better yet, have a member read it, giving you the opportunity to hear your words. And don't forget, you need not adhere to any advice you receive. It's your book.

Over-writing, over-thinking, or how to totally screw up a good story.

With today's economy, it would be expensive and cumbersome to print every version of our writing. We have the capability of saving files on our computer after each write, but it's tedious to go back and re-think the work. Nevertheless, writers are inherently insecure.

The more we receive rejection or criticism, the greater our doubts. The first reaction is to fix it. Does someone order us to do this? Did you receive a long critique, giving you the information needed to revise? Probably not.

We tend to correct, over-correct, slash, kill, hack, chop, over-think, self-degrade, wear out erasers, wear the paint off of the Backspace and Delete keys of our computers, over-develop, under-rate, over-describe, under-mine our work and shoot ourselves in the foot with or without the cliché. In first-person, God voice, or narrative, it makes no difference. You wrote it – therefore it sucks.

Take a romance novel for example. The writer can over-think, whittle, chop, slice and dice and here are the results:

She said yes — he died.

Remember Tom Clancy's advice?

"Keep at it. The one talent that's indispensable to a writer is persistence. You must write the book, else there is no book. It will not finish itself. Do not try to commit art. Just tell the damned story."

Here is my short-list of editing reference musts:

The Elements of Editing – A Modern Guide for Editors and Journalists. *Arthur Plotnik*

Self-Editing for Fiction Writers – *Renni Browne and Dave King*

Revising Fiction – A Handbook for Writers – *David Madden*

The Chicago Manual of Style – The Essential Guide for Writers, Editors, and Publishers – *The University of Chicago Press*

From Microsoft Word we have the handy Review Tab. We can select the 'Changes and Show Markups' choices. This is confusing at first, but stay with it, it's of great use in editing your work, or for others to edit with you.

How important is editing? Like we said earlier, do you want to hang on to the idea once they receive and read your book, a publisher will be so impressed and inspired they will demand to edit and publish it? Probably not. Must you read and correct your work more than one time? Absolutely. Why? They receive more than enough quality submissions near ready for print.

They are eagle-eyed at spotting a professional manuscript and query. (The letter you send asking an editor or publisher to look at your work).

An editorial source claims that it requires two quality readings and edits of galleys (a galleys is a proof of your book your publisher sends to you to review, make changes, or approve). Maybe at this point in the process, 99% of the errors have been corrected. The remaining 1%? These could mean the loss of millions of dollars in sales if one teensy little mistake is made, like misplacing a zero in $1,000, making it $10,000. Keep this thought foremost in your mind as you review your work.

For example: This book contains 13,400 words. One wrong character or space could spell financial disaster if it involves your profit/loss, and a major embarrassment to you. What if you've misspelled names?

Of course you will use your spell/language checker, dictionary and thesaurus. Read out-loud, put your manuscript to bed and reread it with fresh eyes, but DO NOT allow errors to remain in your work. It speaks for you in a positive or a negative way. It sets apart the amateur from the professional.

The Dumpster

Mark Twain once said, "Sometimes you must kill your darlings."

And yes, this is as difficult as it sounds!

Say you describe what Johnny did at the playground in great depth, but it has nothing to do with the little girl who's lost. Your descriptions may be powerful; you share the color of daffodils and your reader can savor the pungent scent of springtime in the park through your evocations, but if little Johnny's play time isn't important to the story line, you must send it to the dumpster.

Make a file and name it Notes, or Dumpster, and hide your orphaned darlings there to use if appropriate at another time.

EXERCISE SIXTEEN

With regard to your story, read and edit, then answer the above 15 points.

How do you feel about getting your story edited?

How do you feel about joining a workshop?

Have you killed any darlings?

"You can always edit a bad page. You can't edit a blank page."   *Jodi Picoult*

About the Author

Jan received her education in Boston. A former acquisitions editor with Fireship Press of Tucson, she is a founding partner of Loose Leaves Publishing of Tucson and Rook's Page Publishing.

A wanderer throughout life, she has lived in MA, CA, IA, NM, CO, WY, TX, AZ, SC and MN. She and her husband Bob, along with their cat (and a fish named Buddy) have returned to the beauty of the Rocky Mountains of Colorado. She enjoys painting, exploring and traveling.

Other Books by Jan

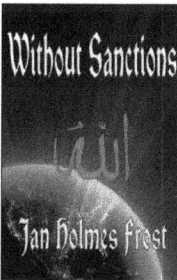

Without Sanctions, is a popular government techno thriller. Will Drexel Rose get ahead of terrorist cells bent on wreaking havoc across the USA?

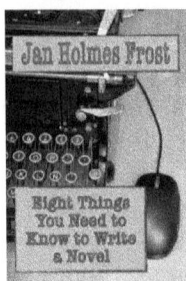

Eight Things you Need to Know to Write a Novel, is taken from workshops and conferences she taught in Texas, California and Arizona. The nuts, bolts and hints every writer wants to have sitting on their desk.

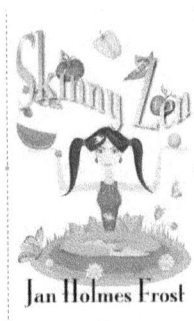

Skinny Zen, is a fun way to set new goals in dieting and a mindful healthy life-style.

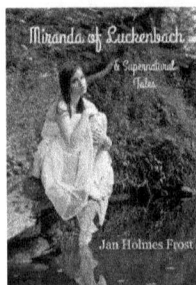

Miranda of Luckenbach & Supernatural Tales women young and old will love these three ghostly stories filled with mystery and fun.

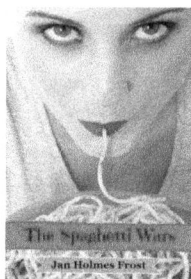

The Spaghetti Wars – Friendship, a failed marriage, and a Boston Italian eatery are stirred together with a heaping ladle of mystery, humor and romance. Every gal must read!

First in the new series: The Pasta Chronicles

Coming next: ***Unravioli***

Contact at: RimeQuillPub@gmail.com

Find all of Jan's books at www.Amazon.com or www.janholmesfrost.com